PARENTS
Train Your Children
In the Way They
Should Go
JENNA JOSINA

Jenna Josina

PARENTS

Train Your Children in the Way They Should Go

Jenna Josina

Christian Publishing House

Cambridge, Ohio

Unless otherwise stated, Scripture quotations are from American Standard Version (ASV) Public Domain

PARENTS: Train Your Children in the Way They Should Go by Jenna Josina

ISBN-13: **9798736661336**

Table of Contents

PARENTS: Train Your Children in the Way They Should Go

Hi friends, my name is Jenna, and I work in the Children's Ministry. I have my undergrad from Pacific Life Bible College and my Masters from Okanagan Bible College. God placed children's ministry on my heart while I was in my early twenties, and I'm still in love with this ministry today. I began working in children's ministry at a small church where I oversaw a handful of kids while also completing my undergraduate degree. From there, I took a quick break while working in a transition house with women and children fleeing domestic abuse, but my heart was still for children. Soon after, I had the opportunity to join a local church, where I am happily still on staff and overseeing their children's ministry programs.

In recent years, I have sensed the importance of spiritual practices in the lives of children. Now, if you don't know what spiritual practices are, spiritual practices are simply ways of connecting with God. Prayer is a spiritual practice, reading your Bible is a spiritual practice, and so is worship. Each of these practices enriches your daily life as you walk with Jesus. However, it is not without a struggle to invite your kids into everyday practices. It can be overwhelming to try and figure out where to start. How do you teach a child to pray? How can you invite your kids into serving? Where do you begin with trying to help your kids grow in the fruit of the spirit? Where do you start with teaching them the Bible stories? How do you teach them to be merciful? Friends take a deep breath. First of all, you can trust that God is at work within your children. Secondly, I'm here to help through the pages of this book.

This book is broken down into three sections: Prayer Practices, Bible Practices, and Everyday Practices. The purpose of this book is simple. It is to help kids grow in a deep and beautiful friendship with Jesus.

Perhaps, as I write this book, I am starting the most important journey of my life in ministering to children... as I expect my very own baby soon.

SECTION ONE Prayer Practices

Praying for Your Children

I wanted to begin simple (not simple as in unimportant, because this practice is essential). But simple, as in, it can be done daily by you. If you are reading this book, it could be safe to assume that you are already praying for your children. But have you thought about what you are praying for?

One of my good friends said that she would always pray that her daughter would be kind to teachers and that she would listen. I had never thought about praying for a child in that way, but the Bible does tell us to pray about everything (Philippians 4:6-7).

I don't think that you can pray in a wrong way for your children. If you are praying for them, then God is going to honor those prayers and listen to you (of course, this doesn't mean you'll get what you want necessarily, but He will hear you). Prayers are answered according to God's will and purposes, not according to our will and purposes.

As I pray for my unborn child, I pray for two things. The first is that my child will be healthy, that there won't be any health challenges, and that my child will be born as perfectly as a baby can be. My second prayer, and far more critical prayer, is that my baby will come to know Jesus. I pray that from the moment my child is born that my child will be introduced to God through those that surround my child, and that my child will never turn away from God. I pray about these two things because they are my two biggest fears. I fear that my baby won't be healthy (or worse, that I miscarry), and I fear that my child will turn away from Jesus. Do you ever pray out of fear?

I think it's ok to pray out of fear because it also shows what's important to us. But what if we expanded our minds, what if we, instead of praying from our fear, started praying for their character. What if we prayed for their future, for their relationship with Jesus, and their friendships? What if we decided to pray into our children (instead of just praying for them)?

Friends, as you begin to read this book, take time to reflect. How do you pray for your children? Take time to decide what you value and pray into the character of your child.

Prayer Song

As I write this next section, I write it with a heavy heart. I did miscarry my child. One of my biggest fears came true, but also one of my biggest hopes. My child is with Jesus.

There is an old song by the Taize Community called, O Lord Hear My Prayer. It's a simple song, but I find it incredibly powerful in my own spiritual life and the spiritual life of the kids in my program. Together we would sing out the lyrics and spend time praying together. The song goes like this...

"O Lord, hear my prayer,

O Lord, hear my prayer;

when I call, answer me.

O Lord, hear my prayer,

O Lord, hear my prayer;

come and listen to me."

Together we would sing the lyrics over and over again, but in-between the lyrics, we would name things we were thankful for, praying for, sad about, wanted to see God's mercy in, or places where we trusted God. The song would go something like this...

"O Lord, hear my prayer,

O Lord, hear my prayer;

when I call, answer me.

O Lord, hear my prayer,

O Lord, hear my prayer;

come and listen to me.

Thank you for my best friend

O Lord, hear my prayer,

O Lord, hear my prayer;

when I call, answer me.

O Lord, hear my prayer,

O Lord, hear my prayer;

come and listen to me.

Help me to trust you when I'm scared at night

O Lord, hear my prayer,

O Lord, hear my prayer;

when I call, answer me.

O Lord, hear my prayer,

O Lord, hear my prayer;

come and listen to me.

I know you are good, even when people are mean at school."

Our song was beautiful, but it also brought a spiritual depth that was undeniable. Not a single child chose not to participate; instead, together, we sang, and together we prayed.

Music can move us. I still find that some of my deepest prayer times are moments where I can also worship through music. It's as easy as turning on the radio to my favorite Christian station and letting the worship lead my prayers. Often, I think about how worship music can move kids too. Kids can praise God with their whole hearts during worship, they can often find the highest highs and the lowest lows during worship, and they too can pray through song.

Prayer in Nature

A quote by Mother Teresa says, "We need to find God, and he cannot be found in noise and restlessness. God is the friend of silence. See how nature - trees, flowers, grass- grows in silence; see the stars, the moon, and the sun, how they move in silence... We need silence to be able to touch souls." I believe this to be true. I need the quietness of stargazing. I need the sound of the ocean waves. I need the sight of bunnies hopping through the grassy fields. I need the shade of a great oak tree. All of these things bring me closer to Jesus. All of these things bring me to my knees and point me to our heavenly Father.

I started playing a prayer game with the kids in my program, we'd play eye-spy, but then we would turn it into our prayer. I would lead the kids to the window and get them to point out what God had created. As they would point things out, we as a class would thank God together. It was a lot of fun, but it also helped the kids to notice creation. It would go something like this, "Look at that tree! Thank you, God, for that tree," or, "I see a doggy, I think God made dogs too. Thank you, God, for that dog," to, "Look at that bug on the window! Thank you, God, for the bugs." It was amazing what the kids could see! It was a good practice to show kids that we don't always need to sit with our hands folded and our eyes shut to be able to pray. It reminded the kids that we can do more in prayer than just ask for the things we need, and it opened the kid's eyes to seeing nature as something God had made.

Our fun eye-spy prayer game wasn't the only way we prayed in nature. One hot summer evening, I took a group of middle school girls on a nature walk. They each had a list of things they needed to find, from rocks, birds, pine trees, and butterflies. The girls were off; they were making a race out of it! It was fun to participate with them, seeing the joy they were having in discovering the nature around them. By the end of the evening, they were rolling down a hill and picking wildflowers. It was such a joy. Before they left, we talked about what they saw and how God had created it all. Then we said a simple prayer of thanks.

There are so many ways of inviting kids to pray through nature. You could go on a hike or a nature walk, and every time you see something amazing, unique, or breathtaking, you simply take the time at that moment to thank the Lord. You could spend more time outside, doing activities like camping, canoeing, horseback riding, or simply walking, and during these times, you could point out the beauty that God has made.

In the spring, I love gardening. You could invite your kids to garden with you. Gardening brings new life. It brings new flowers, new bugs, which bring new animals. We are given new life through Jesus, and gardening is a beautiful time to explain this to your children. You could sit with them in the dirt, pouring water onto the soil, talking about how God has made us new in Jesus. You could sit under a tree and remind your children that Jesus died for our sins on a tree. You could move rocks away from your garden, and you could invite your kids into a conversation about the stone being rolled away and about how Jesus is alive again. Take time to use the world around you, the world God has created, to teach, to pray, and to point your little ones back to Jesus.

Gratitude Prayer

As a child begins their prayer life, most of the time, it's centered on themselves. They ask God for the things they want, the things they need, or any other words their parents tell them to say. It's not deep, and it's not meaningful. Not to say this isn't a real or authentic prayer, it very well could be, but it's a selfish prayer. They are praying only for themselves (and a lot of the time only in hopes that they'll get something out of it). I remember a friend of mine shared a story about her daughter. She was disappointed when her brother was born because she wanted a sister. One day, she decided to ask her mom if she would have another baby. My friend explained to her daughter that she would not. She then went on to tell her mom that she would just need to pray that God would put a baby in her mom's stomach so that she could have a sister. We laughed, and we laughed, but it gave the perfect example of how children pray.

So how can you invite your child into praying with a grateful heart? There are so many fun and creative ways to help kids understand the world around them and invite them to pray outside of themselves. In our last section, we talked about prayer in nature. This is a great place to start. Begin by inviting them into thanking God for the world around them.

A dear friend of mine invites her kids to name things they are thankful for at the dinner table each night. Before they eat, they each take a turn talking about their days at school and what brought them joy. Then, before they would eat, they would thank the Lord for the food before them and for the things they were thankful for throughout their days. I absolutely love this idea; it helps kids realize that all good things come from God.

Another way to invite your kids into a gratitude prayer is by having a journal or a special jar. Every time your kids have something they are grateful for, write it down in the journal or on a piece of paper and place it in the jar. Then, take a moment to pray with your kid and thank the Lord for his good gifts. When your child is having a bad day, take that journal or jar out, and reflect with your child on what has brought them joy in the past. Talk to your child about how God is still good, even when we have bad days.

I also believe that worship can direct our hearts towards gratefulness. Worship can be like a mirror. It can show us our heart, it can help us repent, and it can turn us back towards God. I know that kids worship with their whole hearts. I've seen it. I've seen kids bellow out the lyrics and raise their hands. There are so many great worship songs that are appropriate for kids, don't be afraid to have worship at home or worship time as a family. Invite and encourage your kids to worship God. This, too, can redirect their hearts and help them to be grateful to God.

Friends, it doesn't necessarily matter how you invite your child into gratitude. The important part is that they do recognize the goodness of God and that they have grateful hearts. God has been incredibly good to us, so don't be afraid to share your own stories of God's goodness with your kids. It could make all the difference to them.

Lament

"For this gird you with sackcloth,

lament and wail; for the fierce anger of Jehovah

is not turned back from us." – Jeremiah 4:8

Lament is found throughout the Bible, from The Old Testament to The New. Books like Jeremiah, Lamentations, and Job are full of lament. But Jesus himself also lamented. One of the most tender moments in Scripture is when Jesus finds out that his dear friend, Lazarus, has died, and he takes time to cry. Jesus brings his friend back to life, but not before taking time to lament, as the Bible says, "Jesus wept," (John 11:35), which is one of the shortest verses in Scripture.

Lament is so common in Scripture, yet it's uncommon in our everyday life. We, as adults, are out of practice with lament, which means that we don't often create the space for kids to lament. So, before we begin, let's talk about what lamenting means.

Ann Voskamp says this about lament, "Lament is a cry of belief in a good God, a God who has His ear to our hearts, a God who transfigures the ugly into beauty. Complaint is the bitter howl of unbelief in any benevolent God in this moment, a distrust in the love-beat of the Father's heart." Lament is the moment when we are tempted to turn away from God because of our pain, but we then decide to turn towards God and turn our pain into worship. Lament is when we cry out to God with our whole hearts clinging to our hurt and our need for God. Lament is when we remind ourselves that God is good and trustworthy but that our pain is too much to bear on our own.

Friends, I would invite you to participate in lamenting yourself. I know that lament was an important part of worship for me after my miscarriage. I cried out to God every day for months, desperate to know why I had lost my baby, desperate to feel God's presence, and desperate to know God's voice in the fog. God was with me, and soon my lament turned into worship. God had not forgotten me.

The next time you are feeling heartbroken or in pain, friends turn to God and cry out to Him. God invites you into lament, and God invites your kids into lament also.

I know a group of girls who feel in themselves to be misfits. Either they have a tough time with school, or they don't make friends easily. Some of them struggle with bullies, and others have no friends at all. I find it incredibly heartbreaking that these girls feel out of step because each is so lovely and so lovable. I wanted to create a space for them to feel known and loved. It was springtime, and I was thinking about clay pots. I felt like God wanted me to tell them about how they were clay pots. "Seeing it is God, that said, Light shall shine out of darkness, who shined in our hearts, to give the light of the knowledge of the glory of God in the face of Jesus Christ. But we have this treasure in earthen vessels, that the exceeding greatness of the power may be of God, and not from ourselves; we are pressed on every side, yet not straitened; perplexed, yet not unto despair; pursued, yet not forsaken; smitten down, yet not destroyed;" (2 Corinthians 4:6-9). I was reminded of how fragile clay pots can be, and we, like clay pots, are also fragile. We lament because clay pots can break. We are afflicted but not crushed. We are afflicted, and so we lament.

I believe that each of these girls could lament the loss of friendship and the sadness they go through each day at school. They can cry out to God; they can tell Him about how mad and sad they are feeling about not fitting in. They are going through real hardship, but they are not forgotten, and God is close to them. As they cry out to Him, He will comfort them. In the same way, your kids face hardship. Perhaps it's something big like the loss of a grandparent, or maybe they, like the girls, are also not fitting in at school. Perhaps they are being bullied, or maybe they are very anxious. It could be that they're sad when you leave for work, or something as small as not being able to play because it's raining outside. Whatever it is, your kids can lament.

To begin with, help give your kids words. Perhaps they repeat after you, or you invite them to say how they feel. You can pray like this, "Lord, we're very sad today, we wish that there were more friends at the playgroup. Help us find friends, hear our cry, and remember us in our sadness," or, you could pray in this way, "God, we know you are good, so please come to our aid. Our hearts hurt so much, and we need you to carry this burden for us." As they grow, and as they practice lamenting with you, a habit of lamenting should arise in them, and soon they will be able to cry out to God on their own.

Praying for Others

"May I remain steadfastly faithful to God when my heart is completely broken, and it seems as though my entire world is caving in on me." – Edward D. Andrews

My heart breaks so completely for those who don't know Jesus. I've cried, I've prayed, and I've done everything in my power to show them God's love. Yet, there are times it feels as if I am throwing out dead seeds onto dry ground.

My heart aches for those who are sick, for those who are dying. A seven-year-old boy is too young to have cancer. A teenager who has never learned how to talk. My dear friend, who is in her mid-twenties and who will be sick all the days of her life. I cry out to God, begging Him to remember them.

My heart tears for those who are weary. I can feel my heart shatter as I sit with the abused. I feel sick to my stomach with the one who feels like they have no purpose in this world. I cry alongside those who are too tired to keep going. I call out to God, asking once again for His mercy.

Rarely have I seen a miracle. Only once to my memory have I seen someone physically healed in an instant, yet it doesn't hinder me from prayer. I think I spend more time in prayer because I don't often see healing come to pass instantaneously. We don't serve a vending machine God; we don't put our prayers in and see the results we want coming out. Instead, we serve a God with who we have a deep and rich relationship with. We talk to Him, we cry with Him, and we invite Him into the places where we hurt. We don't always get to understand the workings of our awesome and holy God, but we are always invited into conversation with Him. For this, I believe in petitioning through prayer.

Now, as amazing as they may be, kids have a natural tendency to lean towards selfishness. Depending on their age, there is truly little they do for themselves and almost nothing they do for others. Friends, this is ok. Kids are learning and growing every day, but there is a time early in their lives where thinking and praying for others can be a difficult skill for them. So then, how do you invite them into petitioning through prayer?

Pope Francis developed the five-finger prayer, a simple tool that helps kids pray on their fingers for the people around them. You begin the prayer with your thumb, the thumb is the finger closest to your heart, and so you pray for those you love the most. Your kids can pray for their siblings, for their grandparents, for their friends, and for you! Next, we stick up our pointer finger, and we pray for those who point us in the right direction. This is where we pray for our teachers, our pastors, and our coaches. Then, we hold up our middle finger, our tallest finger, and we pray for those in power. We pray for our government, our health officials, and our leaders. After this, we move on to our ring finger, which happens to be the weakest finger. On this finger, we pray for those who are ill, for those who are poor, and for those who don't know Jesus. Finally, we remember our small finger, which (for small children) reminds them of themselves. We now pray for our own needs. I love this simple prayer. It's easy enough to pray through every day.

There are, of course, other ways to help your children pray for those around them. You could simply help them to become observant. Where I live, we have several people struggling with homelessness. What if you and your child prayed for people struggling with homelessness as you pass them in your car or on a walk? It could be as simple as saying, "see that person on the corner, they aren't doing well, they don't have a home. Let's pray for God to remember them. God, we pray that you remember this person. They aren't doing well. God, we know that you care about them. We pray that you provide for them, amen." Soon, your kids might start joining you and offering up their own prayers. Or, perhaps you pray every time you hear the sounds of a fire truck or an ambulance. You could say, "kids' the sound of an ambulance reminds me that someone needs help, let's help them by praying for them. God, we don't know who is sick, but you do. We pray that you remember them and that you help them in their hour of need, amen." Inviting your kids to pray through everyday life experience creates genuine compassion and awareness in your child, and it gives them a way to voice their concerns to The King of Kings and the Lord of Lords.

Perhaps you would rather make a game out of praying for others. Maybe, you write names of the people in your child's life on popsicle sticks, and you stick them all into a jar. Each day you ask your child to pull one name out of the jar, and each day you pray for that one person. I like this idea because it gives your child time to ask questions about that person and why they should pray for them. Maybe they never knew that aunt Suzie was having dental surgery, or perhaps they didn't realize that their friend Melissa wasn't a Christian. Each day they are given the opportunity to think and ask questions about someone they love, and then they are given a chance to pray for that person. Not only is this prayer game fun, but it creates a real sense of care in your child.

You could also pray for others by giving a world map or a globe to your child. You could pin down where the missionaries from your church are located, and you could pray for them weekly. This would allow you to talk about other countries' needs, places where there is extreme poverty, a dislike of Jesus, or where people don't have homes. It can be challenging for a child to imagine a place unlike where they live, but kids can grow such compassionate hearts for others in the world if they are given the opportunity. You could also use a different colored pin to point out the countries who have the least amount of food, who are in the greatest amount of poverty, who are at war, who have overpowering governments, or who don't allow people to speak about Jesus. Invite your kids into praying with God for the places in the world where they desperately need His help.

Friends, these are only a few ways to invite your kids into praying for others. I know that you can come up with far more ideas but having a starting place can be helpful. Your kids can learn how to love deeply, they can become compassionate, but most importantly they can become real prayer warriors.

Prayer of Examen

The prayer of examen is one of my favorite prayers. I do, however, wish it had a different name. The word examen seems to carry some negative connotations, whereas this prayer isn't the least bit negative. The prayer of examen slows you down, it helps you reflect, and it gives you time to look back and see where God was at work within your everyday life. The prayer of examen is like a mirror. It reflects on your day.

When you begin the prayer of examen with your kids, have them all tucked into bed and ready for a good night's rest. Then, as they are feeling at peace, invite them into prayer. Begin by saying hello to God, "Dear God," or, "Hello Jesus." Next, ask them to say thank you to God. They could thank God for the blue clouds, for their favorite song on the radio, or for their dog (whatever they would like). Once they have spent time thanking God, invite them to start thinking about the gifts God has given them today. Perhaps they saw a flower for the first time this spring, or maybe a friend shared their favorite color crayon. Maybe they got to spend extra time at the playground, or they saw a frog at the pond! Each day we are given gifts. Thank God for the gifts you were given today.

After this, take a moment to pray over your kids. In this quiet moment, invite God to remind your kids of their day and show them how He was with them throughout the day. Then, begin to recall the day by asking them questions, "Do you remember waking up?" As they begin to think back on their day, begin to ask them where God was with them throughout the day, "where was God when you were playing on the playground?" or, "Could you sense God's presence while in music class?" You can talk about the joyful moments, and you can talk about the sad moments. Then, invite your kids to talk about how God was with them in the joy and how God was comforting them in the sadness.

As you come to the conclusion of your prayer, invite your kids to ask God for the grace they will be needing for tomorrow. Invite them to ask God to be close with them, to give them the grace they'll need for others, and for the heart to serve Him.

The prayer of examen is a simple prayer, yet such a powerful prayer. I find that on the nights that I go through this prayer that I feel closer to Jesus. It can be easy to go about our days without recognizing His presence, but God is with us. God is always with us. The prayer of examen is a simple way of helping your kids realize the presence of God in their lives.

The Lord's Prayer

"Our Father who art in heaven, Hallowed be thy name. Thy kingdom come. Thy will be done, as in heaven, so on earth. Give us this day our daily bread. And forgive us our debts, as we also have forgiven our debtors. And bring us not into temptation but deliver us from the evil one. For if ye forgive men their trespasses, your heavenly Father will also forgive you."[1] – Matthew 6:9-14

---

[1] Prayers in the Bible are all example prayers; they are not meant to be prayed from memory, repeated again and again. They are examples of how to pray, what to pray for, and sometimes what emotions should be involved in prayer. Most know of the Lord's prayer in Matthew 6:9-14. In the Lord's prayer in Luke some 18 months later, Jesus, upon the request of the apostles to teach them how to pray, kindly repeated the essential points of that model prayer but

As we end our section on prayer, take a moment to look back on what we have learned. There is so much joy in walking alongside your children and their prayer life. One of the most beautiful things in the world is the bud of a flower during the beginning of spring. In the same way, your children are starting to bud in their relationship with Jesus.

I decided to end on the Lord's Prayer because this is the prayer that Jesus gave us as an example to pray from. It's a simple prayer, yet it can be incredibly profound. Kids, too, can learn from Jesus' wisdom and leadership, so let His words lead our thoughts now.

As we begin, we pray out, "Our Father in heaven, hallowed be your name," hallowed means holy. We begin by praising our holy God. You can invite your kids to praise God by praying out what they love about Him. They could say something like, "God, I love that you made the big tall trees," or, "Jesus, you are so good." Invite your kids to name what they love the most about God and encourage them in praising Him. Kids can be so creative, and so let them be creative in their praise. Perhaps they say, "Thank you, God, for elephants because they make me laugh," this might sound silly, but God made elephants and He made laughter too!

Next, we read, "Your kingdom come, your will be done, on earth as it is in heaven." When I pray for God's kingdom to come and His will to be done, I like to tell kids to pray about what is breaking their hearts. I explain that if it's breaking their hearts, then it's probably breaking God's heart too. Perhaps they want to pray for those without homes or those who don't have enough food. Maybe it breaks their hearts to see bullies at

---

not word-for-word, which meant Jesus was not giving a liturgical prayer to be recited by rote. (Luke 11:1-4) Things that should concern us in prayer: our loving heavenly Father's name (his reputation reflected by us), the kingdom of God, the will of the Father, in heaven and on earth. Our daily needs, forgiveness for our sins and how we should be forgiving others, help with our sinful nature, and protection from Satan, the wicked one.

school, or it could be that a sick grandparent is making them feel sad. Whatever it is, invite your kids into praying for God's will to be done.

As we continue, we move into a time of asking God to provide us with our needs, "Give us this day our daily bread." Kids can be very aware of their needs, perhaps they feel like they need friends at school, or maybe they need food as they are growing. Kids could need more time to rest or help to get all their homework done. I love letting kids express their needs because sometimes they name things that I would have missed. I wouldn't have considered that kids need help from God with going to daycare because they miss their moms, but for some kids, this is a very real need that they need to be able to express. Invite them to express and pray for all of their needs.

"And forgive us our debts, as we also have forgiven our debtors," this, friends, is where we move into a time of confession. There are times that kids know exactly what they need to confess, but there are other times where they don't realize their sinfulness at all. As a child, I was always scared of telling God about the bad things I had done, but I decided to try praying one day. This is my first memory of praying, but what was more impressed upon me than my confession, was the great amount of love I felt from God that day. Kids can feel God's presence, kids can feel God's forgiveness. We don't want to deny kids the experience of fully knowing God, and so confession is an important part of their prayer life. Their prayers could be as simple as, "God, I'm sorry for yelling at mommy," or, "Jesus, please forgive me for not playing nicely today," but God receives each prayer, and each confession is met with His grace.[2]

---

[2] Of course, our children need to understand that God only forgives those who are genuinely repentant (sorry and remorseful) for what they may have said, done, or failed to do.

Finally, we end our prayer in this way, "And lead us not into temptation, but deliver us from evil," as we ask God for protection. I know for myself this is a very important part of prayer, I know how weak I am, but I desperately want to be with Jesus forever. Kids don't always understand our weakness as humans, so often, this part of the prayer feels uncomfortable or unnecessary for them but invite them into it anyways. If they would like, have them repeat after you, "God, please keep us safe from the evil one," or, "Jesus, protect us, we know that we are weak. Keep us from evil." Find your own words but press into God's protection and grace.

Friends, I hope you found this section on prayer practices helpful. My prayer for you is that these practices would enrich the spiritual life of you and your children. Let's now turn the page as we explore Bible reading practices together.

SECTION TWO Bible Reading Practices

Theology and Story

There is such deep importance in teaching the Bible, it deepens our understanding and relationship with God, and it creates refinement in us that we cannot get from anything else. I am choosing to begin this section with Theology and Storytelling because I believe each is important. Kids need to hear the stories of the Bible. They need to hear the story of Abraham, Isaac, and Jacob. Kids need to see the faithfulness of God throughout Israel's history, and they need to realize that Jesus was the promised rescuer. There is a rich history, there is poetry, and there is wisdom. We get to read letters, accounts, and prophecy, and hearing the stories is just as important as understanding them theologically.

I think the best way for me to explain this to you is to give you an example. I remember once watching a video-based curriculum with kids that included everything (it started with worship, it told the story, it went onto the application, and it even included a prayer and a memory verse). Churches could quite literally press play and have their kid's program covered from start to finish. I wouldn't recommend a program like this for a number of reasons, one being the lack of personal investment and discipleship given to the kids, but you also don't have control over what is being presented. In this video we were watching, we were being told about the story of the ten lepers (Luke 17) and how only one of the lepers came back to thank Jesus. It was all going well until we came to the application. The video concluded that we should thank our moms and dads for everything they do for us. I was dumbfounded. They couldn't honestly believe that this story's conclusion was to thank our parents, was this story not about a miracle? Was this story not about the one who came back praising God and thanking Jesus?

When I think about the stories I am telling, I take time to think over what is most important for them to hear. Let's take creation as an example, I story-tell the story of creation, and then at the end, I explain that God made the world and everything in it and that God made us special (this is the theology that I teach, I don't create an application). Another example is when I tell them the story of Jesus healing the blind man. I end by saying that he healed the man so that the man would know Him. In this way, I am not adding in an application that doesn't match the story, but I'm teaching them its purpose.

I often like to remind myself that applications are not always needed, but theology is. I don't need the Bible alone to teach kids good morals or manners. As Christian parents with a biblical worldview, the mind of Christ, you would be called to do this. The Bible is here to enrich our lives and to teach us how to follow Jesus. Let's layaway our cookie-cutter applications, and instead, let's invite our kids into the stories of the Bible and the warmth of its theology.

Storybook Bibles

"When we run from God, we run away from everything that makes us alive and free. We run away from our own happiness. We leave our place where we belong—close to his heart." – Sally Lloyd-Jones (Author of The Jesus Storybook Bible)

One of my friends once joked and said that my favorite things in the entire world were children's storybook Bibles… she wasn't wrong. I love seeing what God-gifted authors have created and crafted together in order to help kids know God better. I believe in the wisdom of these authors, and I believe that Jesus allowed them to write storybook Bibles so that kids could cling to His heart. After all, we know that Jesus loves the little children.

The reason I wanted to include a section on children's storybook Bibles was simply that I wanted to go over the advantages and disadvantages of these amazing tools. Like I said above, storybook Bibles are a gift from God, but they are still a man-made tool, and so we should treat them as such.

It's interesting how different storybook Bibles are written from different perspectives and with a weight of importance in different areas. For example, some storybook Bibles are packed with stories but hold very little theology. On the other hand, there are theologically rich storybook Bibles that miss the entire history of Israel. When my mom was growing up, it was especially important at the time to teach kids about Israel and their history, my mom's storybook Bibles (which she still has), were filled to the brim with details of the Old Testament. Nowadays, you can buy storybook Bibles that are slim on the Old Testament but are rich in theology and point towards Jesus.

Along the lines of what the storybook Bibles contain, you also find that the perspective of the story changes. For example, the story of Noah's ark is one of sorrow. However, it's often told to children as if it's simply about animals upon a boat. There are storybook Bibles that try and create a relaxed or a softer version of the Bible. On the other hand, other storybook Bibles value the rough and toughness of God's word, and they don't try to smooth it down.

Friends, don't overthink it. Your storybook Bible is probably lovely. But it is interesting to think about what your kids are learning from each of these different storybook Bibles. As your child grows, I think about what they need at the stage of life they are in. I wouldn't suggest giving your two-year-old a theologically rich storybook Bible with graphic details of the stories, but I do, however, think your twelve-year-old could handle it.

Friends, my challenge to you in this section is simple. Find out what's important to you for your child to learn and to be hearing at this stage of their life, research a storybook Bible, and choose one that fits. Perhaps you want them to learn that Jesus is our rescuer, or maybe you want them to hear the story of Israel. Perhaps they need something that simply keeps their attention, or maybe they are ready for something with more details. You know your child best. You know what they need. Just be aware that each storybook Bible is different, and each teaches differently. Friends, I hope you have a wonderful time journeying with your child through the world of children's storybook Bibles.

Imagination Prayer

Friends, I could not be more excited to be introducing you to one of my favorite Bible reading practices, Imagination Prayer. The reason I love imagination prayer is that it's the act of imagining yourself in the Bible stories. You get to think through what it would have been like to be standing on the streets of Jerusalem, you can gaze your eyes upon Jesus as he approaches you, and you get to picture the sights, sounds, and smells that would have been surrounding you.

Picture this. You are with a crowd on a beautiful sunny day sitting beneath a tree, hiding from the heat. Your feet are sore, and so you place your feet in the grass. What does the grass feel like against your feet? Ahead of you, you can see the prophet, Jesus. You have heard about this Jesus doing wonderful miracles, and today you sit on the hillside to hear him speak. Can you see Jesus? What is he wearing? Can you see his face? What is his expression, is He smiling, or does He look serious? As the day goes on, you start to become hungry. Can you feel your stomach rumbling? You wonder to yourself why you didn't bring any food to eat? You debate going home, but you are wanting to hear more of what Jesus is saying. You see a little boy walk up to Jesus. What does the boy look like? How old is he? What is he wearing? The boy offers Jesus his simple lunch, and Jesus smiles down at him. Can you see Jesus smiling? Jesus takes the lunch, which happens to be two fish and five loaves of bread and prays. Then Jesus instructs His friends to hand out the food. You watch in bewilderment. What are you thinking? Does Jesus really expect this small lunch to feed such a great crowd? But as you watch, the food somehow doesn't run out. In fact, you are handed as much bread and fish as you could imagine. How could this be? What are you feeling? Are you amazed, are you in disbelief, or are you in wonder? This truly was a miracle of Jesus!

What did you think of that reading? Were you able to imagine and picture yourself under that tree and seeing that miracle? Imagination prayer is a practice that helps kids put themselves in the shoes of those who lived during the Biblical times. Now, I should explain that this practice does take some preparation, and sometimes it can be quite a bit of work. I believe that you can buy books with pre-written imagination prayer stories, but I always love writing them myself. As you begin writing, ask yourself how you would be feeling and what you would be experiencing along the way, then write those questions and experience into the story.

As I begin Imagination Prayer with the kids I work with, I always get them to close their eyes and lay on their backs. Sometimes I can see them starting to act out the story. If we were talking about being hungry, some of them would put their hands on their tummies. If we were talking about feeling the grass on their feet, some would put their feet on the ground. For most kids, this was an experience that worked well for them and that let them experience the story. For a few kids, this practice didn't work at all (and that's ok). Since I work in a classroom setting, I would allow kids to choose to draw the story instead of imagining it, but if you are doing this practice at home, if it doesn't work for your kids, then don't worry, there are other great ways to invite your kids into experiencing the word of God.

Friends, I love this fun practice! I love experiencing it even in my adult life. I hope that this practice can help you and your kids feel closer to Jesus.

Godly Play

"Children have an innate sense of the presence of God. The Godly Play approach helps them to explore their faith through story, to gain religious language and to enhance their spiritual experience through wonder and play." – Godly Play Foundation

Truthfully, I am pretty new to Godly Play, and I tend only to use it one-on-one and not in large groups. The idea of Godly play is to invite kids to use their imaginations to experience the Bible stories. When I first tried Godly Play, I was hanging out with a child who wasn't very interested in knowing God. I pulled out a single piece of paper and a pen, "let's play a game," I said, "I'm going to draw something, and you need to guess what I'm drawing." He loved playing games, and so he was excited to join in. I drew a fence at first, which he guessed after a few tries. Then I drew a tree (which was thankfully a lot easier to recognize than my fence), and then I drew sheep inside of the fence, a shepherd (which again was hard to guess, we can't all be artists), and finally, I drew a sheep outside of the fence. He looked at me and said, "Hey, I know what you're doing, this is a Bible story."

"Is it?" I replied, "which Bible story could it be?"

"It's the story of the sheep that got lost!" He answered excitedly. I had tried to invite him into Bible stories for months, but it was like pulling teeth. Now, this simple activity opened the door for us to talk about Jesus (and he was excited about it)!

Godly play is simple, and you use simple tools (tools that you can find around the house). You can grab little wooden dolls as people (if they're faceless it's best), you can use cotton balls as sheep or as clouds. You could use a blue piece of paper as the sky or as water, and green as the grass. A piece of string could make a gate, or if easier, you could draw it out as I did with the child.

Next, you begin by inviting your child in by using their imagination. Ask them questions about the item you have before them, "what do you think this blue piece of paper could be," or, "look at this cotton ball, what do you see when you look at it?" Have them start to unfold the story with their imagination.

As you go along, you start to add in the details, "you're right, this blue paper is just like water, and this brown cup is a boat. Do you see people in the boat? Who do you think these people could be?" As you go along, you help add in more details, "Yes, that is Jesus in the boat with his disciples. You are right that the cotton ball is a cloud and that the yellow pipe-cleaner is lightning. This is the story of when Jesus calmed the storm."

When preparing for Godly Play, it's important to go over the story a few times on your own so that you know it well enough to tell it through your props. Imagine yourself as a storyteller who is being led by your audience, your kids.

Although I am new at Godly Play, it's a spiritual practice that I quite enjoy! I love letting kids use their imaginations (kids should be kids), and it brings a sense of joy to the story for them.

Act It Out

"Play gives children a chance to practice what they are learning." – Mr. Rogers

I believe that playing is important. It gives kids the chance to imagine, practice, and wonder by using their entire body. I once took a course on helping kids who had a loss in their lives, and one of the most important steps was to invite them into play. Often kids who had seen their parents sick in a hospital would want to play doctor (this gives them a sense of control).

Or kids who had seen something traumatic might want to play a policeman or a firefighter (giving them the sense of understanding of what happened). Therapy is full of play, schools are full of play, homes are full of play, and I believe that churches can be full of play too.

I remember once teaching a grade four class about Easter. After we were done with our lesson, it was time for play. I always include a time of play in our classes because it's how kids connect and build friendships (and I believe it's essential for kids to have friends in church). I watched as a group of boys started to act out the story of Jesus's resurrection - just on their own. They were taking what they had learned, and they were playing the story by acting it out.

There are many Bible scripts online, and every once in a while, I print one out and bring costumes into the classroom. I have each kid pick a character and dress up how they would imagine the person to be dressed. Then, each taking their script, they begin the read through the script and naturally act out what they are reading. It always amazes me how acting out a story can help bring the story into memory. Friends, this is an easy activity to do at home, I'm sure you have dress-up clothes around your house, and kids love any opportunity to play with their parents.

For younger kids (those who cannot read), I often just read from a storybook Bible and assign them a character. They also get to choose their costume, and they get excited about being part of the story. As I begin reading the story, they begin acting out their character (they sometimes need a bit more direction than the older kids, but it's so natural for kids to find a rhythm of play).

Friends, play is good for both the young and the old. This is why we love going to the theatre and seeing stories come to life. We love the adventure of play! We love being invited into a story that comes into action. It brings a sense of excitement and awe. I hope that you and your children have such a sense of joy as you enter into play together!

Bible Investigator

"Thy word is a lamp unto my feet, And light unto my path." – Psalm 119:105[3]

Becoming a Bible Investigator is a practice that I begin with kids who are in Kindergarten. My hope with teaching kids to become Bible Investigators is that they will learn to understand the Bible. When we read storybook Bibles, we often aren't given the context of what book we're reading or its significance. Kids often don't know the difference between a Psalm or a letter in the Bible, yet the Bible is a rich text, and we are invited into knowing and understanding it.

I begin by teaching kids the family tree of Jesus. There are many Jesus family tree pictures on the internet or that are made into posters. We begin with the Old Testament in September and move into the New Testament in December at Christmas. As we begin the Old Testament, we go through Jesus' family tree. I want the kids to understand the promise that God gave to Abraham, see God's faithfulness to Israel, and I want the kids to understand that Jesus is the fulfillment of God's promise.

Next, I found cards online that had each of the books of the Bible categorized under its literary genres. Before starting a new book of the Bible, I would ask the kids to tell me what genre the Bible's book was part of. As they answered, I would give a simple sentence to help them understand the context, "that's right, Proverbs is a book of wisdom, wisdom books aren't giving us promises, they are teaching us wise ways to live," or, "Yes, John is a Gospel, the Gospels are a historical book that

---

[3] In other words, God's Word will guide you with what you are immediately faced with day to day (light to your feet) and with your short term and long term future (light to your path).

really did happen in history. The Gospels teach us about the life, death, and resurrection of Jesus."

Finally, I would invite the kids to ask: Who, What, When, Where, and Why? Not always do the books of the Bibles include answers to all of these questions, but a lot of them give good clues in the first chapter. I would invite the kids to gather as much information as they could as we began learning about a new book of the Bible.

I love going through this process with kids. Kids like exploring the Bible and learning what they can for themselves. This process helps give kids ownership of what they are learning and give them the context.

Life Journaling

Finally, I wanted to end our Bible Reading Practices by talking about Life Journaling. I love Life Journaling; it helps me process what I'm learning with God. In January, our entire church life journaled together (from our children to our seniors), but of course, our little one's life journal much differently than our adults.

When Life Journaling with a toddler or a preschooler, invite them into drawing the story as you read it. What are they hearing? Perhaps they draw a giant fish as you read Jonah, or maybe they draw Jesus as they learn about the sermon on the mount. Whatever it is, let their creativity guide them in the drawing process. Afterward, ask them about their drawing, let them tell you what they learned and what they drew. Kids often have reasons for things, and sometimes it's as simple as asking, "why did you draw a fish?" for them to explain, it was because they thought the fish was scary or that the fish seemed really important. After this, ask them what they learned about God in this story and what they learned about people. At this age, they'll need some prompting (they don't always know what they have learned), but they are often able to engage on some level. Then, spend time praying with your kids.

For those in Kindergarten through Grade four, I like to use S.O.A.P (Scripture, Observation, Application, Prayer). As they are listening to your reading the story, get them to follow along in their own Bibles. When something pops out at them, get them to write that verse down. After you are done reading, invite them into writing out what they observed and what they learned. Then, spend time praying together. If your child doesn't like writing, you can easily ask them these questions instead of having them write them down.

Finally, my favorite age group to life journal with is grade five and grade six. This year I started life journaling with the grade five-six class on a regular basis, and it's been a highlight for me. I've been using the dramatized audio Bible, and it's been a hit! Together, we would pray, and then each would take out their Bibles and their journals as we followed along with the audio Bible. Instead of journaling through S.O.A.P, I would invite this group of kids to journal through S.H.A.P.E (Scripture, Hear, Application, Prayer, Exalt). After we finished listening to the audio Bible, I would play a worship song and I would invite them to spend time with Jesus in prayer and to journal through the text. It was beautiful. So many of the kids expressed feeling close to Jesus in this process.

Life Journaling is a tool that can be used for both kids and adults. Friends, as you read your Bible, perhaps you want to give Life Journaling a try. As you become comfortable with Life Journaling, invite your kids to join you and process the Bible together through writing and prayer.

SECTION THREE Everyday Practices

The Importance of Giving, Caring, Mercy, Fruit of the Spirit, Bible Memory, and Serving

Everyday practices are practices that you do in everyday life. I love this idea because we aren't simply just Christians at church. We are Christians in our workplaces, at our schools, and with our friends. We are Christians in our finances, in our play, and in our sports. Every day I have the opportunity to walk with Jesus in my everyday life. As we begin, let's start by talking about giving, that is, sharing.

We, as adults, give a tithe to the Church as well as offerings. Giving is a way that we participate in worship, but for kids (who don't have an income), giving is not usually part of their everyday life. Giving can be worshipful, and it can help kids understand the importance of financially giving towards God's Kingdom. So how do we invite kids into giving when they don't have an income?

One of my friends invites her kids into giving by fundraising with her kids towards their favorite charities. My friend lets her kids help research different organizations (perhaps your kids have an interest in helping the poor, the elderly, or those who are sick), and she talks to them about the importance of helping those in need. My friend also spends time explaining how God cares for those less fortunate and how we can love them by supporting them. Then, my friend signs them up for a fundraiser and helps them raise money for their chosen organization.

I love the idea of getting your children involved. Another way to get your children involved is by sponsoring a child in a third-world country. You can talk to your kids about how you as a family are helping to support this child financially. There are so many great sponsor child organizations, but I would suggest using an organization that allows you to communicate with your sponsor child. Invite your child into writing them letters and picking out gifts! Your child might not be directly involved in giving money, but they can start to understand the importance of giving money.

I would also encourage you to engage your children in giving at your church.[4] Most people give online or on their credit cards, but many churches still hand around an offering plate. As the offering plate comes around, give your kids money to put into the plate and talk to them about the importance of giving towards God's Kingdom. If your church doesn't have an offering plate, invite them into a conversation around giving towards the church. Teach your children about the importance of giving and show them that you tithe.

One of my good friends encourages her children to give part of their birthday or Christmas money towards a charity. My friend never forces them to give, she just simply asks. Her kids are always willing to give and it brings them great joy to be able to help those who are in need. Her kids get to choose where the money goes, and their compassionate hearts love being able to help others. I absolutely love this because it shows that her kids have hearts towards giving. They aren't being forced. This shows a worshipful heart!

Friends, there are so many ways to teach your kids to give. Your kids are compassionate and kind, and as you invite them to give, their giving will turn into worship.

---

[4] The tithing of the Old Testament is no longer an obligation but giving is an obligation. Jesus and the apostles now expect us to give from our heart. Some can give more than ten percent and other cannot afford ten percent. The one giving more offsets the one who cannot afford to give more.

2 Corinthians 9:7 Updated American Standard Version (UASV)

Each one must do just as he has purposed in his heart, not grudgingly[a] or under compulsion, for God loves a cheerful giver.

[a] Or *reluctantly*

The Importance of Caring

"learn to do well; seek justice, relieve the oppressed, judge the fatherless, plead for the widow." – Isaiah 1:17

Caring for others is important. God cares greatly for people, and we are to care for them also. We live in a broken world, a world where not everyone has food to eat, a roof over their heads, or money to care for their families. Caring for others is an important everyday practice for you and your kids.

I think caring for others can come naturally for kids. Kids often have soft hearts, and they often have a desire for people to no longer be hurting. Perhaps you have a lonely elderly neighbor a few doors down. You could invite your kids into visiting with them or leaving chalk notes on their driveway. Maybe you have a friend who is sick. Allow your kids to help bake them a pie or pick out flowers from the store. Let's say they have a friend at school who is in poverty. Let them choose out toys that they want to give to their friend. Kids love helping people. It's natural for them. Let your kids press into care.

At church, there are opportunities for kids to learn to care as a community. Perhaps your church has a clean-up or gardening day. Invite your kids to come with you and to help clean up or garden around the church. This gives your kids the opportunity to care with your community for the church. Or maybe you have someone in your congregation who is sick, invite your kids to write cards, and pray for the ill person. It can be easy for us to go about our lives without inviting kids into caring for others but teaching kids to care for their community helps bring a sense of ownership and compassion.

Another way to help kids enter into care is by inviting them to care for their grandparents. Often grandparents will need help around the house. You can send your kids over to help change light bulbs, set up their computers, or play a game of chess with their grandma or grandpa. Not only will this bring your parents joy, but it will help your kids understand the importance of caring for those who are older than them.

Along with caring for people, we are also called to steward and care for the earth (Genesis 1-2). Invite your kids to help clean up garbage at their favorite playground or to bike to a friend's house instead of being driven. You can talk to your kids about the importance of caring for the world because God created it, and you can invite them into activities like gardening, setting up a bird feeder, or going for nature walks.

Friends, caring for others, and caring for the world around us is important. Help your kids enter into care by inviting them to love others in their everyday life.

The Importance of the Fruit of the Spirit

"But the fruit of the Spirit is love, joy, peace, longsuffering, kindness, goodness, faithfulness, meekness, self-control; against such there is no law." – Galatians 5:22-23

I once had an entire nine-week series devoted to The Fruit of The Spirit. Each week the kids were assigned a different fruit, and they were to practice that fruit throughout the week. I'm not going to go into details of how I created this series to work, but what was important to me was that the fruit is put into practice (and that the kids didn't just learn about the fruit). I wanted the fruit to be put into practice because that's how we grow in The Fruit of The Spirit.

Friends, you can do this at home. You can either choose to do The Fruit of The Spirit week by week, or you could decide to pick a fruit that your child is struggling with and work on that fruit with them. Think about each of the fruits, beginning with love. How do you teach your child to love God and to love others? Could you invite them into worship at home? Or could you invite them into praying out what they love about God? How about loving others? Could they bake cookies for a friend?

Or could they invite someone over who they don't know very well? Practicing love can be tricky, but the more you practice it, the more you grow in it.

Next is my favorite Fruit of The Spirit, joy! Now, I won't go through all of The Fruit of The Spirit because I know that you can come up with creative ways of teaching your children. But I wanted to pause on joy because, as Christians, living in joy is such an important part of our lives. I love how James 1:2-4 explains that we are to count it all joy, "Count it all joy, my brethren, when ye fall into manifold temptations; knowing that the proving of your faith worketh patience. And let patience have its perfect work, that ye may be perfect and entire, lacking in nothing." In every situation, we are to count it all joy. Now, this can be a hard saying (especially when we're going through a hard time). When I had my miscarriage, I was in lament, and I wasn't thinking or feeling joy, but there was a joy that came out of staying faithful to God through the pain. Inviting your kids to practice joy on the good days will help them to find joy on the not-so-good days. You could do this by naming the things that brought them joy throughout the day, by praising God for his goodness each day, and by becoming joy detectives (finding joy throughout the day). On the not-so-good days, you could choose to remember the joy that God has given you in the past, and you could practice following Him, even when life is hard.

Friends, these are only the first two Fruit of The Spirit, but I know that you are able to take these examples and expand them to all nine of the fruits. The important part isn't learning what the fruits are. It's learning how to press into each one of the fruits and choosing to grow in it. Remember that your kids are still small and are still growing, and God is faithful to them.

The Importance of Bible Memory

Bible Memory is both a tricky practice and a rewarding practice to do with kids. Kids don't like doing anything that they consider hard (or school-like), but in the end, it gives them the gift of having scriptures memorized to heart.

I think it's important to find joy and to have fun with kids. I'm a true believer that play is important, so let's talk about finding the fun in Bible memory! A few years ago, the kids in my program spent the entire year memorizing Psalm 23. Each month we would take on a new verse, and the fun part for them was when they would be able to bring that verse to memory. However, we weren't memorizing these verses with our arms crossed and sitting on the floor. We were building blocks, playing hopscotch, and searching high and low.

One of my favorite ways to help kids memorize Scripture was by writing the verse on Duplo blocks. I would take the Duplo blocks apart, and the kids would need to put them back together in the order of the verse. This was the perfect activity for boys. Boys in Kindergarten to grade two love lego, blocks, and building. I was simply taking an activity that they already loved doing and turning it into a memory verse game. Once the blocks were built, we would then read the verse together a few times. This activity helped the kids think about the words of the verse as they placed the blocks together.

Another activity that we often played was memory-verse hopscotch. I would write the verse on several pieces of paper, and I would tape them to the floor in a hopscotch shape. On one foot, the kids would need to hop from paper to paper while reading out the words of the verse. This was a tricky activity because hopping on one foot and reading at the same time was hard, but it became a challenge for the kids, and they wanted to complete the entire hopscotch. This activity would give them the drive to memorize the verse.

Another way we memorized Scripture was by hiding puzzle pieces all over the room. On the puzzles, I would have written the memory verse, and as they found the puzzle pieces, they would need to put the verse together. They loved this activity because it created a challenge for them to find the pieces and then put the puzzle together.

Friends, you could easily do these activities at home with your kids or could find a simpler way of memorizing Scripture that fits with your family's schedule. Perhaps you choose to memorize a verse every time you walk to school or every time you drive to church. Maybe you decided to put a scripture poster up in your child's rooms for them to memorize on their own times. Or perhaps you choose to go through a memory verse at the breakfast table in the morning. Friends, no matter how you choose to memorize Scripture, make it fun, and invite your kids into the joy of knowing God's word!

The Importance of Mercy

"Mercy and forgiveness must be free and unmerited to the wrongdoer. If the wrongdoer has to do something to merit it, then it isn't mercy." – Timothy Keller

As Christians, we are called to be merciful, but it's no secret that mercy doesn't come easy for children. How do we invite kids into mercy? I believe that one of the most effective ways that kids learn to be merciful is in how they see their parents treating others. Take a moment to think about how you treat others. Are you a person of justice (not that justice is bad, justice is often needed in the right situations), or are you a person of mercy? When you see a person struggling with homelessness, do you cross the street, or do you say hello? When you know someone is sick at church, do you bring them flowers, or do you avoid eye contact? I had a friend whose dad was dying of cancer, and she told me that she hated going to church because people felt awkward about the idea of death, and they would avoid talking to her. Friends, this isn't supposed to make you feel guilty, but to help you become aware. If you want to help your kids enter into mercy, then you need to be merciful.

Invite your kids into conversations about people all over the world, both locally and internationally. Talk to your children about the hardship that people face. As parents, you want to protect your kids, but understanding the world can help your children become merciful. I remember watching the World Vision TV show every Sunday after church as a child, it was my first realization of what poverty was. I was transfixed, I couldn't imagine a world without homes, food, or water, and it helped my heart to become compassionate as a child.

Next, invite your children into caring for those who need mercy. Keep granola bars in your purse or your car and invite your kids to help you hand them out as your cross paths with those who are struggling with homelessness. Invite your kids to write cards, buy flowers, or bake cookies for those who are ill or for those who are lonely. Encourage your kids to visit the elderly and to spend time with people with who they wouldn't normally spend time.

Friends, mercy is a spiritual practice that we can all grow in but inviting your kids into growing in mercy will help them all the days of their lives. We have a merciful God, and we ourselves can be merciful.

The Importance of Serving

Finally, I wanted to end by talking about serving. I believe that serving is important for every person who is part of the body of Christ, including children. Children have the ability to help the church, their families, and their communities. I love seeing children put their faith in action by serving others.

I have a friend who takes her son to the foodbank with her every time she goes to volunteer. This activity enriches her son's life and gives him the ability to serve and to care for others. I absolutely love this idea, I love that they serve as a family, and I love that they invite their son to serve alongside them.

In my program, I always involve the older kids in helping the younger kids. By the time kids are in grade five, they are old enough to start helping out in the nursery and preschool classrooms. Kids love feeling responsible, and even handing out the crayons or helping with the actions to a song can help kids gain ownership and responsibility as they serve God's Kingdom.

The next time you have an opportunity to serve at the church or elsewhere, invite your kids to join you. Kids can pour coffee, they can visit with the elderly, they can care for those younger than them, and they can help stack chairs. It's easy for us to think of kids as getting in the way but inviting them into service (even if it takes us longer to complete our tasks) will enrich their lives and give them an understanding of what it means to serve God and to serve others.

Friends, we are at the end of our short journey together. My hope is that this book was able to give you ideas of how to walk alongside your children in their spiritual lives. We were able to talk about prayer practices, Bible reading practices, and everyday practices. Friends, go in the hope of Jesus Christ, knowing that God loves your children so much.

Bibliography

Ann Voskamp (2011). "One Thousand Gifts: A Dare to Live Fully Right Where You Are", p.175, Zondervan

Author: Taizé Community(no biographical information available about Taizé Community.)

Go to person page. (n.d.). O Lord, hear my prayer. Retrieved March 02, 2021, from

https://hymnary.org/text/o_lord_hear_my_prayer_o_lord _hear#Author

Clare, J. (2017, March 14). 25 quotes about the importance of play. Retrieved April 02, 2021, from https://www.teacherswithapps.com/67552-2/

Kutsu companions: Spiritual direction and Prayer Resources. (n.d.). Retrieved March 26,

2021, from https://bit.ly/2PM6hDD

M. (n.d.). Mother Teresa Quote. Retrieved March 04, 2021, from

https://www.azquotes.com/quote/292124?ref=god-and-nature

Mercy quotes. (n.d.). Retrieved April 05, 2021, from

http://www.notable-quotes.com/m/mercy_quotes.html

Mother Teresa (author of MADRE Teresa. Ven, Sé mi luz Las cartas Privadas de La "santa

De Calcuta"). (n.d.).

Retrieved March 22, 2021, from

https://www.goodreads.com/author/show/838305.Moth er_Teresa

Pope Francis' 5 Finger Prayer. (n.d.). Retrieved March 22, 2021, from

http://uploads.weconnect.com/mce/f90a34bcd66e597a5 d391005bf1e14a7c70f1d2c/RelEdForms/Pope%20Francis%205 %20Finger%20Prayer.pdf

Sally Lloyd-Jones Quotes (author of The Jesus STORYBOOK BIBLE). (n.d.). Retrieved March 31, 2021, from https://www.goodreads.com/author/quotes/92710.Sally_Lloyd _Jones

The Holy Bible: American standard version. (2011). Oxford, UK: Benediction Classics.

The Holy Bible, English Standard Version. ESV® Text Edition:

2016. Copyright © 2001 by Crossway Bibles, a publishing ministry of Good News Publishers.

Thomas, A., & Thomas, A. (2021, March 22). Godly play foundation. Retrieved March 31,

2021, from https://www.godlyplayfoundation.org/

www.ingramcontent.com/pod-product-compliance
Lightning Source LLC
Chambersburg PA
CBHW060917130726
48001CB00006B/2289